Seussical

THE MUSICAL

VOCAL SELECTIONS

Music by STEPHEN FLAHERTY
Lyrics by LYNN AHRENS

David Shiner

Project Manager: Sy Feldman
Cover Art: David LaChapelle
Photos: Joan Marcus
Art Layout: Odalis Soto

The Company

Janine LaManna (front) and The Company

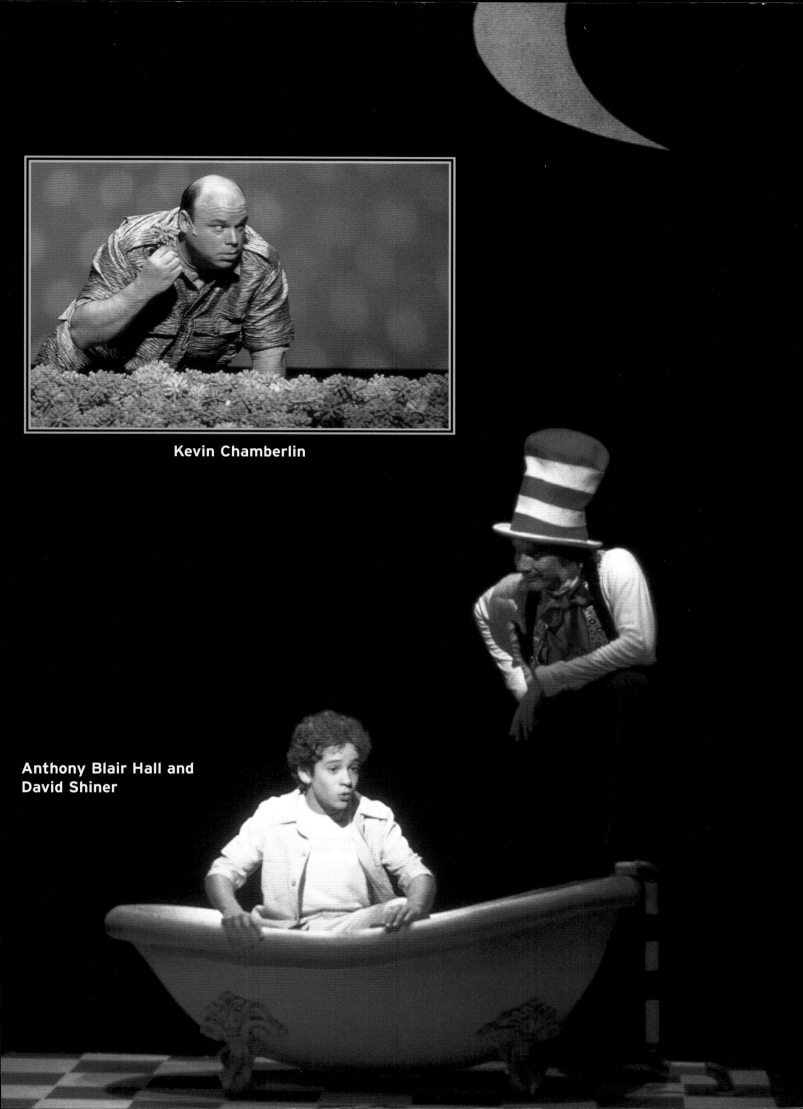

Kevin Chamberlin

**Anthony Blair Hall and
David Shiner**

Kevin Chamberlin (front) and The Company

Kevin Chamberlin, Sharon Wilkins and The Company

A Note From the Authors

When we were approached to write a stage musical based on the works of Dr. Seuss, we were cautious. Although we both remembered loving his stories as children, what would their appeal be for us today? How could so many disparate stories be tied together? What would the musical world sound like? And how would we ever be able to adapt his quirky language and specific rhyme schemes into something varied and theatrical?

We started by doing what our mothers had done for us when we were both kids: we sat down and read the books to one another aloud. To our amazement, the stories seemed fresh and relevant and profound—we suddenly realized that beyond their inspired silliness, they dealt in the most subtle ways with very contemporary themes, from politics to nuclear war. And as we laughed our way through one story after another, rhythms and music began springing to mind, and characters began leaping off the page, begging to be heard. Horton the Elephant emerged as a sympathetic hero, jeered by the other inhabitants of the Jungle of Nool, but loyal and selfless to a fault. Insecure little Gertrude McFuzz demanded to have her "tail" told. We knew the lazy Mayzie and her abandoned egg could play a part. The anarchic Cat in the Hat would wend his way through our story as the audience's "host and emcee." Of course, there were the Whos, people so tiny they live on a speck of dust, and one young Who named JoJo, a "Thinker" of strange and wonderful "Thinks." It seemed to us that here were the main characters and themes for an exciting new musical.

Since the world of Dr. Seuss, by its fantastical nature, isn't based in any particular time, place or reality, we realized there were no limits to what kind of music we could use. Here was a world without rules—a rare opportunity to be completely free. The score emerged as a Seussian gumbo of musical styles, from Latin to pop to swing. For the hip, cool Jungle of Nool, we used elements of gospel, R&B and funk. The tiny world of the Whos seemed to want a sound of its own: marching bands on helium with a sort of "neo Spike Jones" approach. Horton and JoJo were kindred souls—two Thinkers—whose music was more acoustic and lyrical: "Seuss Unplugged." The Cat in the Hat became a "new vaude-villian," blithely humming his way through every grim situation. We even enlisted our brilliant orchestrator, Doug Besterman, to create synthesizer sequences that turned gorillas, birds, elephants, pneumatic drills and other odd sounds into never-before-heard percussion instruments. We tried to filter all of this through our own theatrical sensibility—to carry the story almost entirely in the music.

As for Dr. Seuss' language, the challenge was to weave his idiosyncratic poetry seamlessly with our own words yet stay true to his spirit and ideas, wit and wordplay. Soon we were spinning story titles, character names and snippets of his verse into score, making up our own strange words as we went along; if the characters stopped singing long enough to speak, we decided that they would always speak in verse. It meant a lot to us when Mrs. Audrey Geisel, the widow of Ted Geisel (Dr. Seuss) told us she couldn't tell where he left off and we began. High praise, indeed.

The pure process of writing *Seussical* together was a joy. We had fun. We were free. We drank a lot of coffee and laughed and cried our way into the heart of his magical world. We tapped into our childhoods and brought our adulthoods to bear. As a result, our collaboration of almost eighteen years has grown stronger, and the score is something we're extremely proud of. We hope you'll have a stoo-mendous time in the world of *Seussical*.

Lynn Ahrens and Stephen Flaherty
December, 2000

LYNN AHRENS and STEPHEN FLAHERTY

Lynn Ahrens (lyrics) and Stephen Flaherty (music) have been collaborators in the musical theatre since 1983. Their work has been heard on Broadway, in film, on the concert stage and in theatres across the country and internationally.

Most recently, they wrote the score for *Ragtime* (based on the E. L. Doctorow novel, with book by Terrence McNally), winning the 1998 Tony Award, Drama Desk Award and Outer Critics Circle Award for Best Score and receiving two Grammy nominations for *Songs From Ragtime* and *Ragtime Original Broadway Cast Recording*.

Also in 1998, Ahrens and Flaherty received two Academy Award nominations and two Golden Globe nominations for the songs and score of *Anastasia,* Twentieth Century Fox's first feature animation.

They are the co-creators of the hit Broadway musical *Once on This Island,* which was awarded London's 1995 Olivier Award as Best Musical and received eight Tony Award nominations, including Best Score and Best Book.

Also for Broadway, they wrote the score for *My Favorite Year,* the first original American musical produced by Lincoln Center.

Their musical farce *Lucky Stiff,* first produced off Broadway by Playwrights Horizons, won the prestigious Richard Rodgers Award and Washington's 1990 Helen Hayes Award as Best Musical.

In 1999, Ahrens and Flaherty wrote *With Voices Raised,* a concert piece for orchestra, mixed chorus, tenor soloist and speakers, which was commissioned by Keith Lockhart and the Boston Pops Orchestra and has been performed at Boston's Symphony Hall and Carnegie Hall in New York.

Individually, Ms. Ahrens is the lyricist and co-book writer for *A Christmas Carol,* Madison Square Garden's annual holiday musical. For her work in network television as a songwriter, creator and producer, Ms. Ahrens has received the Emmy Award and four Emmy nominations, and her songs are a mainstay of the renowned animated series "Schoolhouse Rock."

Mr. Flaherty wrote the incidental musical for Neil Simon's play *Proposals* on Broadway. His *Ragtime Symphonic Suite* premiered at the Hollywood Bowl under the direction of John Mauceri, and his musical themes from *Anastasia* were also featured at the Bowl in a "Tribute to the Music of Twentieth Century Fox." He is a founding member of the acclaimed theatre company Drama Dept.

Cast recordings and soundtracks of Ahrens and Flaherty shows are available on Decca Broadway, RCA Victor, Atlantic, Sony, Varese Sarabande and TER, and their music is published by Warner/Chappell. They are members of ASCAP and the Dramatists Guild, where both serve on the Dramatists Guild Council.

CONTENTS

OH, THE THINKS YOU CAN THINK

Music by STEPHEN FLAHERTY

Lyrics by LYNN AHRENS

Brightly ♩ = 120

Oh, the Thinks you can think!

Oh, the Thinks you can think if you're will-ing to try.

Think in-vis-i-ble ink! Or a Gink with a stink! Or a stair to the sky!

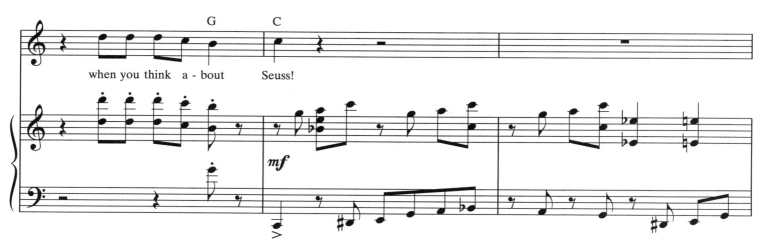

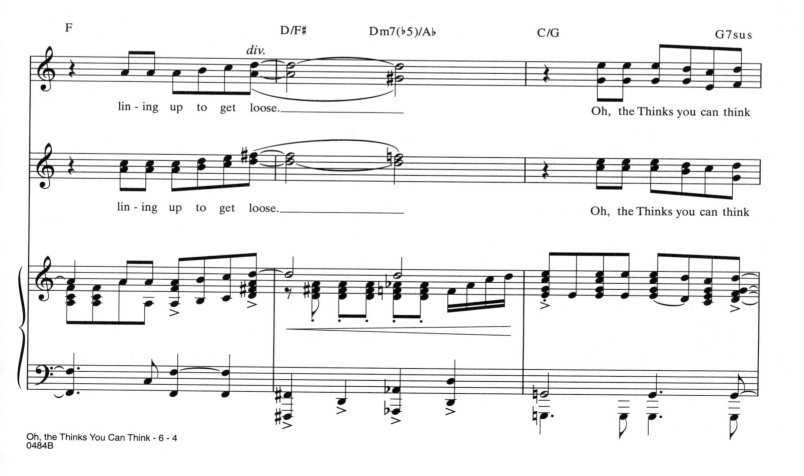

Oh, the Thinks You Can Think - 6 - 6
0484B

HORTON HEARS A WHO

Music by STEPHEN FLAHERTY

Lyrics by LYNN AHRENS
and DR. SEUSS

Horton Hears a Who - 9 - 2
0484B

16

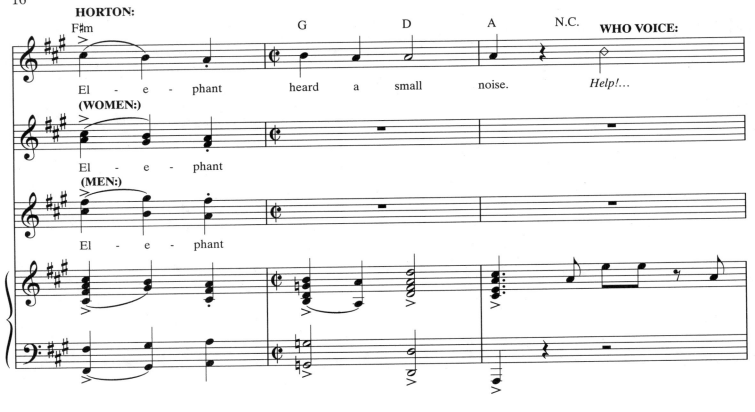

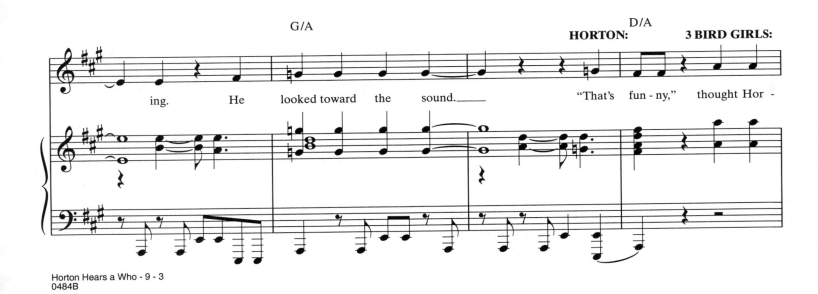

Horton Hears a Who - 9 - 3
0484B

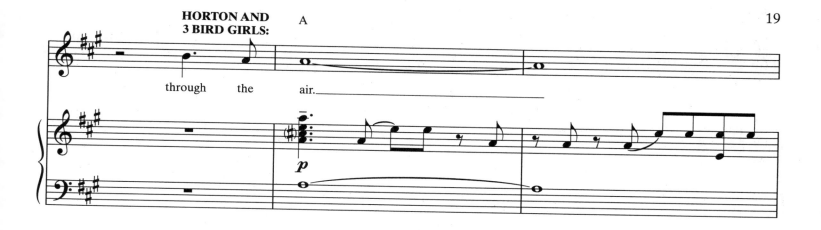

HORTON AND
3 BIRD GIRLS:

A

through the air._____

HORTON:

I say! How con-fus-ing! I

nev-er heard tell of a small speck of dust that was a-ble to yell. So you

know what I think? Why, I think there must be some-one on top___ of that small_

20

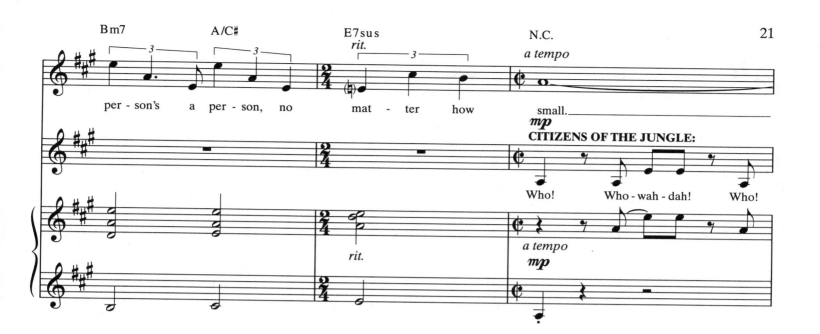

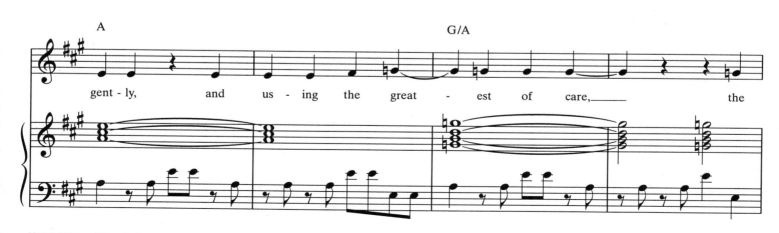

D/A
div.
A
unis.
el - e - phant stretched his great trunk through the air, and he
G/A
G/B
A/C♯
lift - ed the dust speck and car - ried it o - ver and
A/D
HORTON:
3 BIRD GIRLS:
G
D
placed it down, safe, on a ver - y soft
p
A
CITIZENS OF THE JUNGLE:
mf
clo - ver.
Who! Who-wah-dah! Who! Who!
f

BIGGEST BLAME FOOL

Music by STEPHEN FLAHERTY

Lyrics by LYNN AHRENS

24

A DAY FOR THE CAT IN THE HAT

Music by STEPHEN FLAHERTY

Lyrics by LYNN AHRENS

CAT IN THE HAT:
Think of a day— that is rain-y and gray— and as dull as they come. And there is no-bod-y there,— and you're kick-in' a chair— and it's oh so ho-hum! Noth-in' to do— and no-bod-y but you— on a day that is flat-ter than flat. Well,

IT'S POSSIBLE

(McElligot's Pool)

Music by STEPHEN FLAHERTY

Lyrics by LYNN AHRENS
and DR. SEUSS

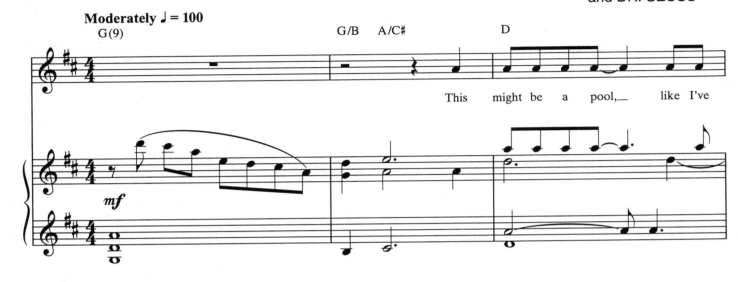

It's Possible - 6 - 1
0484B

36

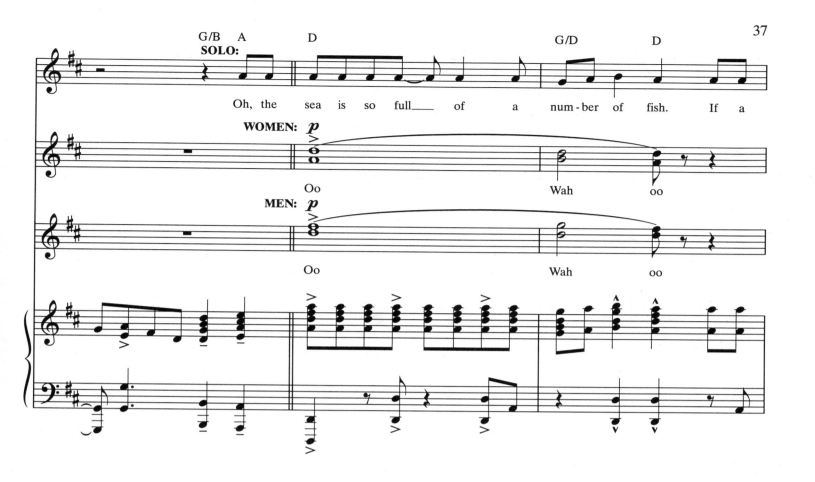

SOLO: Oh, the sea is so full___ of a num-ber of fish. If a

WOMEN: *p* Oo Wah oo

MEN: *p* Oo Wah oo

fel - low is pa - tient, he might get his wish! And that's why I think___ that I'm

Oo Wah oo Oo

Oo Wah oo Oo

THE MILITARY

Music by STEPHEN FLAHERTY

Lyrics by LYNN AHRENS

GENERAL GENGHIS KAHN SCHMITZ:

(Spoken proclamation:) I'm

Gen-er-al Gen-ghis Kahn Schmitz! I scare chil-dren out of their wits. (Sung:) But you'll

see at a glance, sir, my school is the an-swer for shirk-ers and dream-ers and twits. And

til he's mus-cled and tan! A-hut - two - three! *He's pa-thet-ic!* A-

hut - two - three! *Un-ath-let-ic!* A-hut - two - three! But I'm bet-ting we

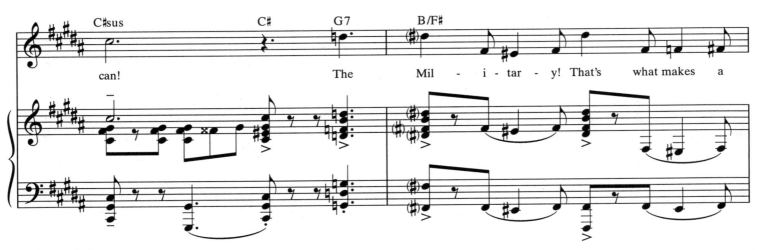

can! The Mil - i - tar - y! That's what makes a

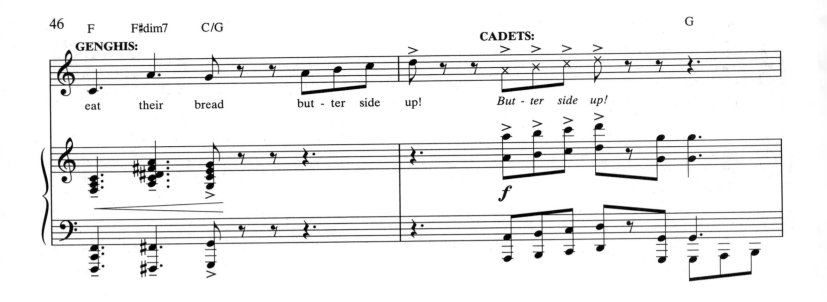

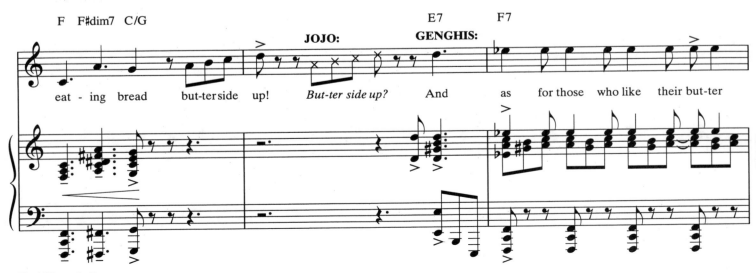

ALONE IN THE UNIVERSE

Music by STEPHEN FLAHERTY

Lyrics by LYNN AHRENS

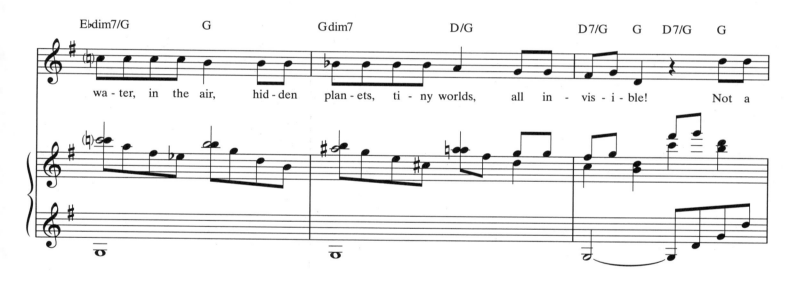

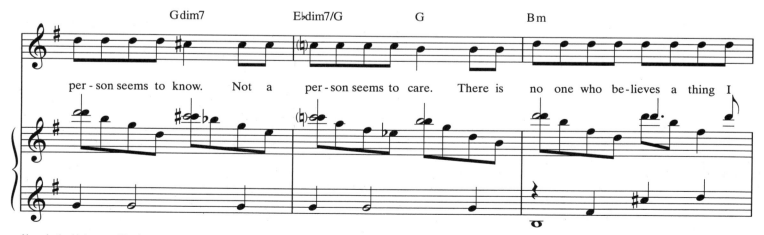

Alone in the Universe - 12 - 1
0484B

54

56

One small voice in the u - ni - verse.

JO-JO: One true friend in the u - ni - verse.

BOTH: Please be - lieve in me.

cresc.

AMAYZING MAYZIE

Music by STEPHEN FLAHERTY

Lyrics by LYNN AHRENS

Bright latin feel ♩ = 112

MAYZIE:
I was once__ a plain__ lit - tle bird like you, kid. One pa - thet - ic feath - er was all I

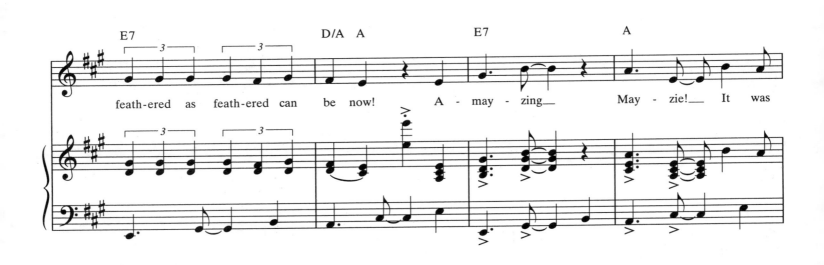

(MAYZIE:)

al - most   as a may - zing   as

me!!!

Zip!!

HOW LUCKY YOU ARE

Music by STEPHEN FLAHERTY

Lyrics by LYNN AHRENS

How Lucky You Are - 4 - 1
0484B

NOTICE ME, HORTON

Music by STEPHEN FLAHERTY

Lyrics by LYNN AHRENS

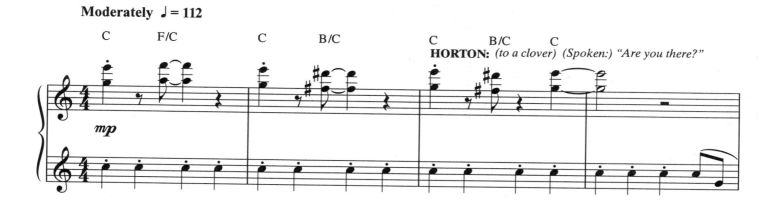

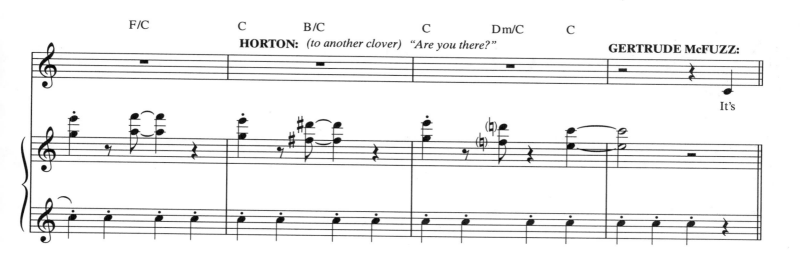

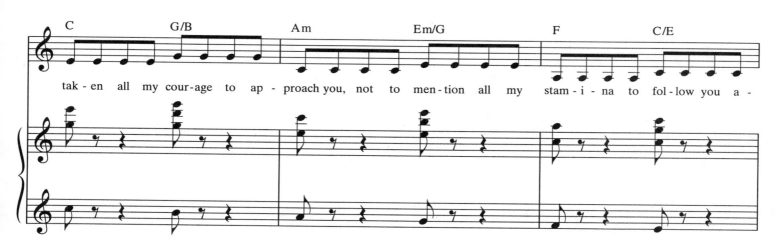

Notice Me, Horton - 8 - 1
0484B

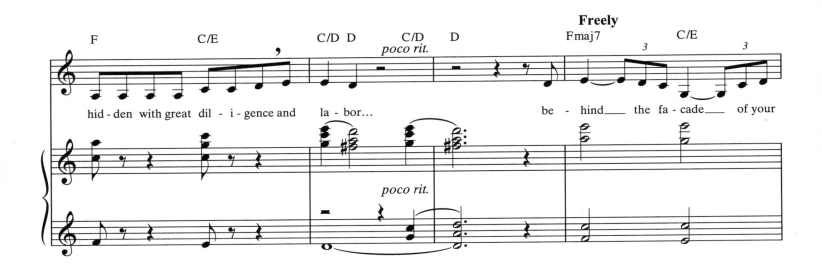

This is your next-door neigh-bor call-ing! No-tice me, Hor-ton.

Hor-ton, to-geth-er, we could be great... Oh,

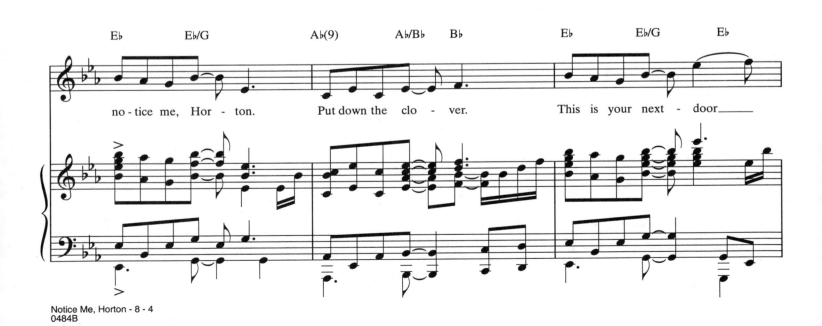

no-tice me, Hor-ton. Put down the clo-ver. This is your next-door

78

You showed up___ and showed___ me some - thing

You showed up___ and showed___ me some - thing

more._____ Now I've be - come___ a some -

more._____ Now I've be - come___ a some -

one who has some - one to be - lieve___ in and to

one who has some - one to be - lieve___ in and to

SOLLA SOLLEW

Music by STEPHEN FLAHERTY

Lyrics by LYNN AHRENS

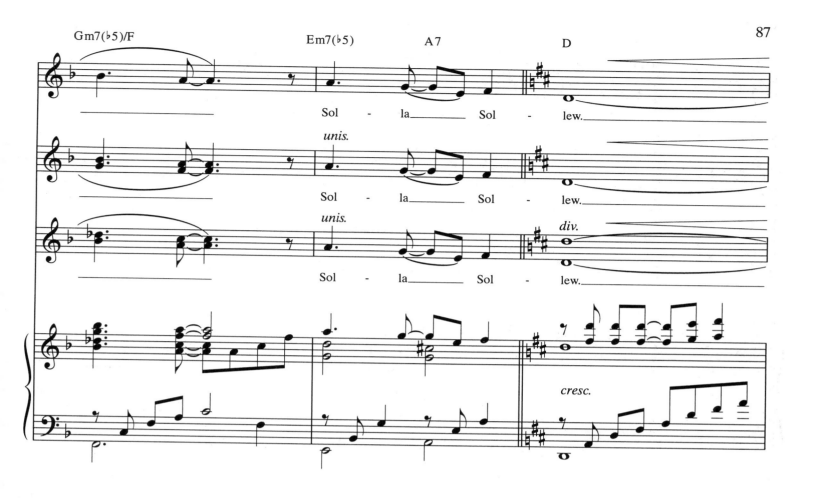

89

on the sea, ___ soon- er or lat - er I'll find it.

I have a pic - ture of how ___ it will be. On the day I

do, trou - bles will be through_____

and I'll be home with you.

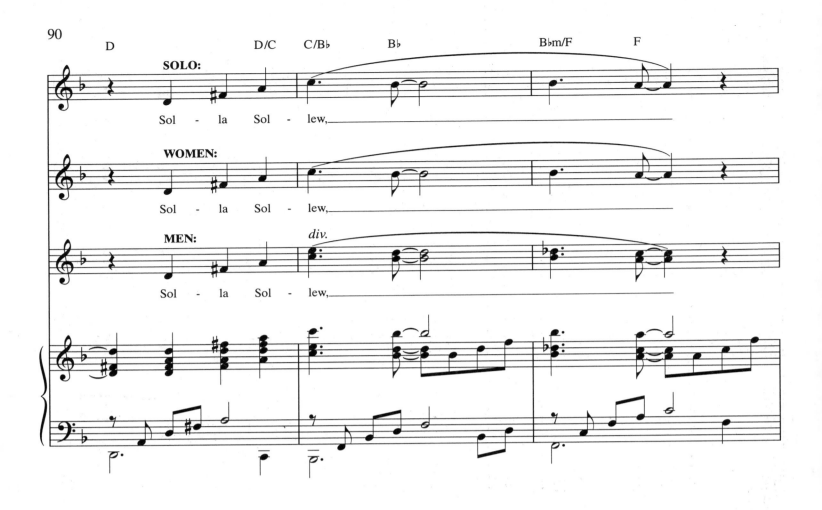

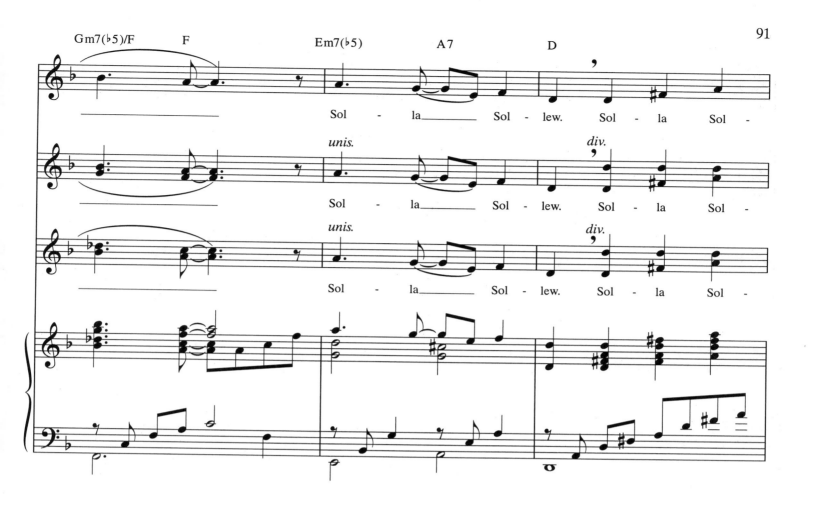

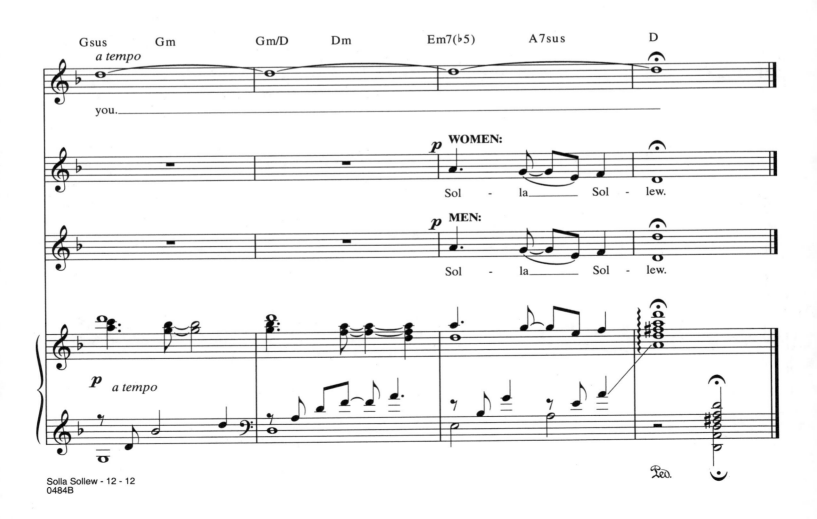

ALL FOR YOU

Music by STEPHEN FLAHERTY

Lyrics by LYNN AHRENS

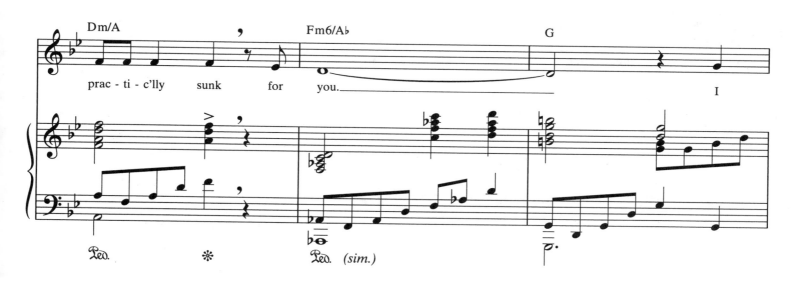

All for You - 7 - 1
0484B

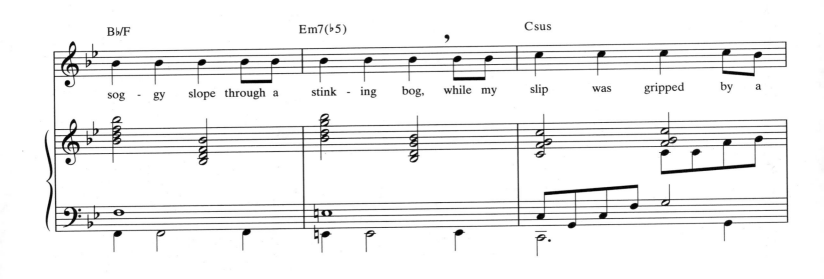

GREEN EGGS AND HAM

Music by STEPHEN FLAHERTY

Lyrics by LYNN AHRENS
and DR. SEUSS

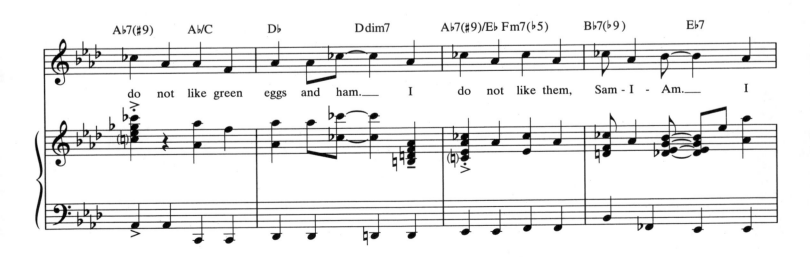

do not like green eggs and ham.___ I do not like them, Sam - I - Am.___ I

Green Eggs and Ham - 4 - 1
0484B

Green Eggs and Ham - 4 - 4
0484B

SFX THEATRICAL GROUP   BARRY & FRAN WEISSLER

and

UNIVERSAL STUDIOS

present

SEUSSICAL THE MUSICAL

Book by	Music by	Lyrics by
LYNN AHRENS and **STEPHEN FLAHERTY**	**STEPHEN FLAHERTY**	**LYNN AHRENS**

Conceived by

LYNN AHRENS, STEPHEN FLAHERTY

and

ERIC IDLE

BASED ON THE WORKS OF DR. SEUSS

starring

KEVIN CHAMBERLIN

JANINE LaMANNA   **MICHELE PAWK**   **ANTHONY BLAIR HALL**

ERICK DEVINE	**EDDIE KORBICH**	**ALICE PLAYTEN**	**SHARON WILKINS**	**STUART ZAGNIT**

ANDREW KEENAN-BOLGER

SHAUN AMYOT JOYCE CHITTICK JENNIFER CODY NATASCIA DIAZ DAVID ENGEL
SARA GETTELFINGER JUSTIN GREER ANN HARADA JENNY HILL CATRICE JOSEPH
MICHELLE KITTRELL MARY ANN LAMB DARREN LEE DAVID LOWENSTEIN MONIQUE L. MIDGETTE
CASEY NICHOLAW TOM PLOTKIN DEVIN RICHARDS WILLIAM RYALL
JEROME VIVONA ERIC JORDAN YOUNG

and

DAVID SHINER

as

THE CAT IN THE HAT

Scenery by	Costumes by	Lighting by	Sound by
EUGENE LEE	**WILLIAM IVEY LONG**	**NATASHA KATZ**	**JONATHAN DEANS**

Orchestrations	Music Director	Dance Arranger	Vocal Arranger
DOUG BESTERMAN	**DAVID HOLCENBERG**	**DAVID CHASE**	**STEPHEN FLAHERTY**

Casting	Music Coordinator	Wig and Hair Design	Press Representative
JAY BINDER & SHERRY DAYTON	**JOHN MILLER**	**PAUL HUNTLEY**	**BARLOW • HARTMAN** PUBLIC RELATIONS

Produced in association with	Associate Director	Scenic Design Coordinator	Associate Choreographers
KARDANA/SWINSKY PRODUCTIONS **HAL LUFTIG & MICHAEL WATT**	**STAFFORD ARIMA**	**LARRY GRUBER**	**ROB ASHFORD** **JOEY PIZZI**

Executive Producers	Production Supervisor	Production Management	General Management
GARY GUNAS **ALECIA PARKER**	**BONNIE PANSON**	**JUNIPER STREET PRODUCTIONS**	**ALAN WASSER ASSOCIATES**

Choreographed by

KATHLEEN MARSHALL

Directed by

FRANK GALATI